790.1
FEB   February holidays
           handbook

DATE DUE

BRODART		07/90 17.27	

Reagan

FEBRUARY HOLIDAYS HANDBOOK

by Ruth Shannon Odor
Dotti Hannum
Annetta Dellinger
Beth Holzbauer
Sandi Veranos
Paulette Glenn
Helen Bauman
Dorothy Farrow
Ruth M. Powell
Kay Wilson

illustrated by Mina McLean

THE CHILD'S WORLD

TIMBER RIDGE ELEMENTARY

ELGIN, ILLINOIS 60120

EDITOR: Sandra Ziegler

Distributed by Childrens Press, 1224 West Van Buren Street, Chicago, Illinois 60607.

Library of Congress Cataloging in Publication Data

Main entry under title:

February holidays handbook.

   1. Holiday decorations. 2. Handicraft. 3. Holidays.
I. Odor, Ruth Shannon, 1926-   II. Ziegler,
Sandra, 1938-
TT900.H6F4 1985   790.1'922   84-15572
ISBN 0-89565-270-6

1 2 3 4 5 6 7 8 9 10 11 12 R 90 89 88 87 86 85

FEBRUARY HOLIDAYS HANDBOOK

USING THIS HANDBOOK

(For teachers of students in grades K-3)

If you teach kindergarten or first through third grade, you will find many ideas in this book to help you chase the winter doldrums from your classroom.

You'll find ideas here to use for Groundhog Day, Lincoln's Birthday, Valentine's Day, and Washington's Birthday. Choose some, and try them. You can mix them together, and create your own exciting month!

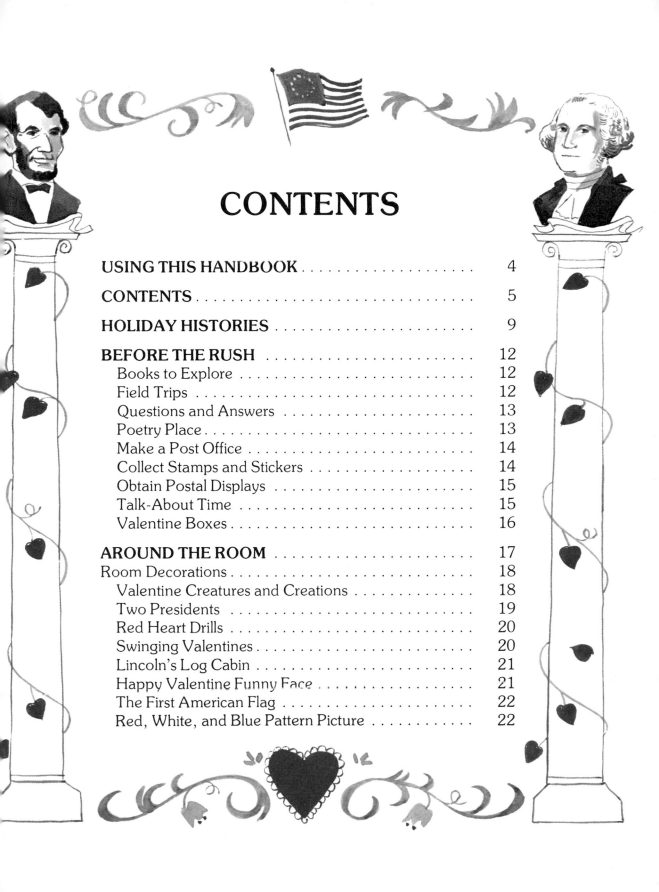

CONTENTS

HOLIDAY HISTORIES

by Ruth Shannon Odor

PRESIDENTS' DAY

In 1968 the Congress of the United States passed a new law. The law changed some of the days that had been set aside by our government as national holidays. The holidays were changed so they would always be celebrated on Mondays. That was so people who get those holidays off at work can have three days off in a row to rest, go on picnics, or take trips.

Among the holidays that were changed were Washington's birthday and Lincoln's birthday. They were combined to make just one holiday. Congress set the third Monday in February as that holiday. Some calendars call that day President's Day. It is a special day for celebrating the birthdays of our two most famous presidents.

Of course, when we celebrate Presidents' Day, we are not celebrating the real birthday of either president. So some states still celebrate the birthdays on the days the men were born.

Abraham Lincoln

Abraham Lincoln was born in a log cabin near Hodgenville, Kentucky, February 12, 1809. He became the sixteenth president of the United States.

"Why don't we make Lincoln's birthday a national holiday?" some people asked in 1891. The next year the State of Illinois (where Lincoln lived for many years) decided to make February 12 a state holiday. Soon other states followed Illinois' example.

Today Lincoln's birthday is celebrated at the Lincoln Memorial in Washington, D.C. It also is observed, with programs, speeches, and parades, in many other places throughout the United States.

George Washington

George Washington was born February 22, 1732. He is often called the father of our Country because he was our first president.

Before he became president, Washington served as the leader of the Revolutionary Army. Then he was known by everyone, especially his soldiers, as General George Washington.

When he was forty-six, Washington and his soldiers were camped at Valley Forge. George's wife, Martha, came to visit her husband on his birthday, and the whole camp helped him celebrate.

After the Revolutionary War, General Washington's birthday became an important American holiday. During colonial days, the people of America observed the birthday of the king of England. The new nation decided to celebrate the birthday of its own famous general. They held balls and banquets, programs and parades.

George Washington's granddaughter, Nellie Custis, was married on his last birthday, February 22, 1799, at Mount Vernon.

VALENTINE'S DAY

Valentine's Day was named after a man known as Saint Valentine. But, as many as seven or eight different men were called Saint Valentine. So today we aren't sure for which person Valentine's Day was named.

A story about one such person says that the Roman emperor ordered young men not to get married. He thought that if they were married, they would not want to leave home to fight in wars. It is said that a man named Valentine felt sorry for young couples in love and married them secretly.

Another story, or legend, says that once, while a man named Valentine was in prison, the jailer's little blind daughter became his friend. Valentine prayed for her, and she regained her sight. Before he died, he wrote her a letter, and signed it, "From your Valentine."

Still another legend says that a man named Valentine raised flowers and gave them to children. But one day he was put into prison. Because the children missed their friend, they picked flowers, tied notes to the bouquets, and tossed them through the window to Valentine. After Valentine was killed, people began to send written

messages or flowers to their friends on the anniversary of his death, February 14. They called these gifts and messages, "valentines."

BEFORE THE RUSH

(Preparation Ideas)

Here are some ideas to think over before February comes. They will help you celebrate the February holidays in a variety of ways.

BOOKS TO EXPLORE

Below is a list of some stories and books that you may want to use during February. Check your local library for these and other holiday books your students will enjoy.

- *Our Valentine Book*
- *Wise Owl's Birthday Colors*
- *Magic Monsters Learn About Weather*
- *Learning About Love*

- *George Washington: A Talk With His Grandchildren*
- *Survival at Valley Forge*
- *The Valentine Box*
- *A Birthday for General Washington*
- *A New Flag for a New Country*
- *Arthur's Valentine*
- *The Hunt for Rabbit's Galoshes*
- *One Zillion Valentines*
- *Best Valentine in the World*

For a catalog from The Child's World, write to P.O. Box 989, Elgin, Illinois 60120.

FIELD TRIPS

Before Valentine's Day is here, you may want to plan a visit to a post office, candy factory or store, bakery, florist, or card shop, so your students can find out what is done in preparation for Valentine's Day.

QUESTIONS AND ANSWERS

(Second and third graders will especially enjoy this activity.)

At the beginning of the month, have each student write one question he or she has regarding Valentine's Day, George Washington, or Abraham Lincoln. Collect the questions and redistribute them. Provide a variety of resource materials on the three topics so that students can research their questions and find answers. Plan a sharing time when questions and answers can be read aloud by students.

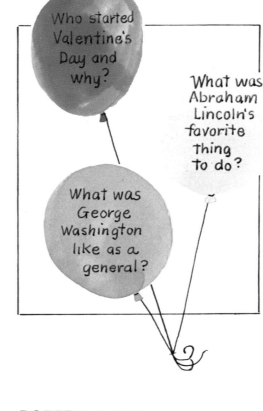

POETRY PLACE

Select and read some February holiday poems to your class. Then invite students to write their own poems on the following topics: Groundhog Day, Valentine's Day, George Washington's Birthday, Abraham Lincoln's Birthday. Let the pupils draw pictures to illustrate their poems. Share the poems and pictures with the entire class. Then display the students' creative pieces on a classroom wall or bulletin board.

MAKE A POST OFFICE

Early in February, set aside an area of the room to be a post office. Build the pretend post office from a large packing box. On the back of the box, cut out a door. On the front, cut a large window to fold back and use as a postal counter. Make openings for mail slots below the large window, and label them "LOCAL," "AIRMAIL," and "SPECIAL DELIVERY." Secure a shoe box behind each slot to catch the letters.

Next obtain a shoe box for each student. Assign one name to each box, and arrange them in order as postal boxes within the post office.

Encourage children to bring their valentine cards into class a few days before Valentine's Day. They may drop the cards into the slots at their post office. Allow several children (acting as postal workers) to sort the mail, putting it into the proper boxes. On Valentine's Day, have several others take turns delivering the cards from the postal boxes to the children's desks.

COLLECT STAMPS
AND STICKERS

In advance, collect various kinds of stamps and stickers to be used in

the pretend post office. Let the children sort the stamps and classify them by sizes, colors, designs, etc. Talk about any commemorative stamps in honor of Washington, Lincoln, or Valentine's Day.

OBTAIN POSTAL DISPLAYS

You may want to obtain some displays from your local post office, or by writing to the United States Postal Service, The Postmaster General, Washington, D.C. 20260.

TALK-ABOUT TIME

Plan to order something for Valentine's Day by mail. Keep track of how long it takes to receive your order. (Also see page 29.)

Here is a basic mailing sequence:

1. Write an order.
2. Put an address on the envelope.
3. Put a stamp on it.
4. Mail the letter in a mailbox.
5. A mail carrier will pick it up and take it to the post office.
6. The letter will go by plane to the post office where you sent it.
8. A mail carrier will deliver the letter to the right address.

VALENTINE BOXES

Collect a variety of scrap materials for students to use in making Valentine boxes. Provide things such as detergent and milk containers, paper plates, drinking straws, toothpicks, yarn, paper and fabric scraps, empty thread spools, etc. Tell students to use their imaginations in constructing unusual Valentine boxes. Suggest that the boxes be constructed and decorated to look like favorite objects, pets, boats, spaceships, robots, cages of lovebirds, castles, etc.

AROUND
THE
ROOM

ROOM DECORATIONS

VALENTINE CREATURES & CREATIONS

Children may make many Valentine creatures and creations using red, pink, green, and white construction paper; scissors; crayons; and glue. Some examples are shown here to help you get them started—be creative!

by Dotti Hannum

Mortimer Mouse

Valentine Forget-Me-Not

Heart House

Red

White

brown →

Red

White

Love Bug

Red Hot Dog

½ Heart

Teddy Turtle

Jenny Giraffe

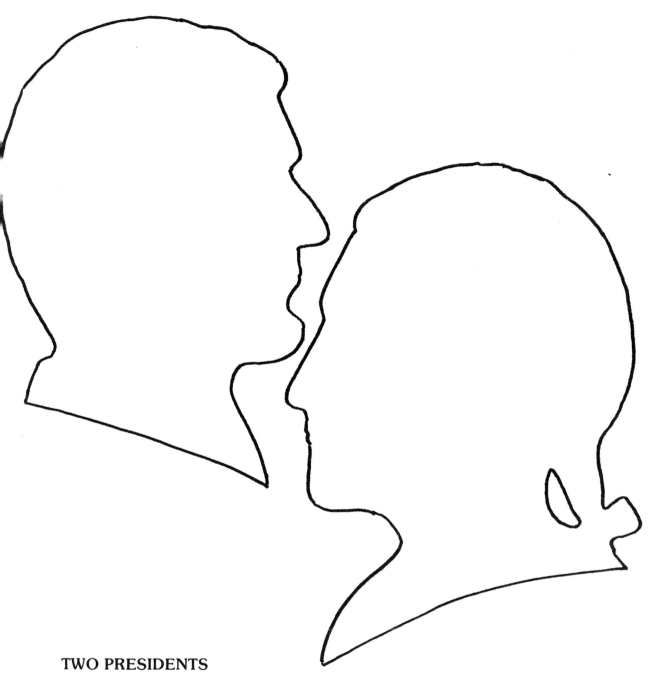

TWO PRESIDENTS

Use the patterns on this page to make cardboard patterns. Let older students make red silhouettes of Washington or Lincoln. Each pupil should glue his figure on white construction paper and cut it out again about one-quarter inch wider. Then he should glue the figures on blue construction paper and repeat. Hang the silhouettes in the room.

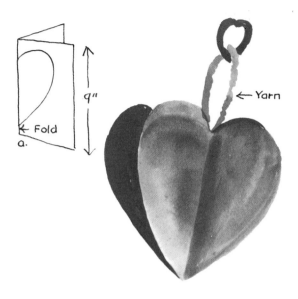
← Yarn

q"

← Fold

a.

RED HEART DRILLS

Cut a large red flannel or felt heart. Attach it to poster board or a bulletin board. From various colors of flannel or felt, cut numerals, shapes, colors, and so forth. Let the children use the pieces to practice their counting and recognition skills.

SWINGING VALENTINES

Tell the pupils to choose two colors of construction paper (red/white; pink/white; red/pink). Demonstrate as you explain. Fold each sheet in half. Place one inside the other. Cut a heart on the fold. (See illustration a.) When you finish, you will have two different-colored identical hearts.

From the scraps, cut two identical small hearts the same way. Glue the small hearts back to back to make one heart. Then cut a heart shape from the center of the glued heart, and throw the shape away.

Insert a piece of yarn through the glued heart to make a hanger.

Glue one half of each large heart together, back to back, with the yarn hanger between them. Open the unglued halves so you have a three-sided swinging valentine. If desired, you may decorate each of the three sides before you hang the valentine.

LINCOLN'S LOG CABIN

You will need 9-by-12-inch sheets of white or light blue, brown, and black construction paper, scissors, glue, and crayons.

The pupil should cut the brown paper along the 9-inch side to make eight or ten strips. He should glue the strips, one above another, on the white or light blue paper to shape a cabin.

Each pupil may cut a roof out of black paper to fit his cabin and glue the roof above the top log. He may also cut a door and window out of the black paper. Glue them on.

Each pupil may draw and color scenery around his log cabin. If he wants, he may add a chimney out of paper scraps, or draw one with a crayon.

Use the pictures to decorate the room.

HAPPY VALENTINE
FUNNY FACE

Let the students cut hearts from construction paper. While the hearts are still folded in half, older students may cut noses and mouths in them. (See illustration.) To cut eyes, they draw a small heart on the still folded hearts, above the nose and over a bit. They fold hearts again so they can cut out heart-shaped eyes on the fold. Let students open the valentines and see the funny faces. Use the funny faces to decorate the windows.

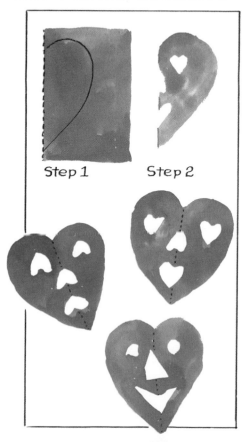

Step 1   Step 2

THE FIRST AMERICAN FLAG

After you tell the story of Betsy Ross and the first American flag, let the children make these colorful paper banners.

For each flag, you will need one 9-by-12-inch sheet of white construction paper, seven 11/16-by-12-inch strips of red construction paper, and one 5-by-6-inch piece of blue paper, scissors, glue, white chalk, or thirteen small stick-on stars.

Each pupil should glue seven strips of red paper on his white paper. If the pupil leaves a space between each strip, he will end up with red and white stripes.

Each student should glue a piece of blue paper in the upper left corner of his flag.

He may draw thirteen stars in a circle on the blue paper, or put thirteen stick-on stars in a circle on the background.

RED, WHITE, AND BLUE PATTERN PICTURE

In honor of the birthdays of Washington and Lincoln, make blow-through-a-straw pictures, using the colors red, white, and blue.

You will need 9-by-12-inch sheets of white construction paper, red and blue tempera paint, and straws.

Let each child drop small blobs of red and blue tempera paint on a sheet of white construction paper.

The pupil should blow through the straw, aiming at the paint puddles. This will make the paint move about in interesting patterns. He should keep blowing until the picture looks almost like fireworks!

When the pictures have dried, they will look especially attractive if mounted on red or blue background paper, or on a bulletin board covered in red or blue.

BULLETIN BOARDS

OUR VALENTINE HOUSE

Ask each child to bring a family picture to school. (If students do not have pictures, you may want to have everyone draw his family.) Decorate the bulletin board to look like a house (see illustration). Use cardboard or paper shingles for the roof and brick crepe paper or construction paper for the chimney. Divide the house into rooms, using paper strips or yarn for dividers. Add pictures as on illustration. Put a construction-paper door in the center. Use the caption: Our Valentine House. Discuss families; talk about how every child's family is different, and yet special. Help the children understand that families may live in different kinds of homes. Both at home and away, family members may do many different kinds of jobs. Families are a good place for us to learn to give and receive love. Leave the Valentine House up for several weeks. The children will love to take their friends to see the board.

by Annetta Dellinger

MY SPECIAL VALENTINES

Ask each child to bring a school photo of himself to class.

Have the children glue their pictures onto white or red paper doilies. (Or students could cut red hearts from construction paper and glue their pictures onto the hearts.)

Use a contrasting color (white, red, or pink) to make a wide border around the bulletin board. (Use ribbon, crepe paper, or a purchased border.) Then attach the pictures.

In the center of your board place a large heart (cut from red construction paper or cardboard) that says, "I love you."

Above the heart put two cupids shooting their bows and arrows.

Fill the board with hearts and arrows (some pointed towards the children's pictures).

by Beth Holzbauer

THE ALPHABET STORE

Tell the children about how Abe and another young man borrowed money and used it to buy groceries and supplies to sell in their own store. Later, Abe decided to study to be a lawyer. His partner ran the store. Instead of selling the groceries, the partner spent his time eating and drinking. Finally he died, leaving the store in debt.

The store and its contents were sold at an auction. But still there was not enough money to pay all the debts. Abe Lincoln owed more than a thousand dollars!

"Honest Abe" worked hard as a lawyer. Finally he earned enough money to pay back every cent.

Move from this idea to making a bulletin board store.

Cover the board with white paper. Put a narrow brown border around it so it looks like a store window. Hang a sign in the window, "The Alphabet Store." Cut out pictures of items Lincoln's store might have sold—one for each letter of the alphabet. Mount the pictures on construction paper. On three-inch paper circles print the alphabet in

capitals; on two-inch circles print the lower case letters. Place tacks, the circles, and pictures near the bulletin board. Let the children hang pictures of things for sale "in the store window." Beneath each picture, the children should fasten the capitals and lower-case letters that begin the names of the items in the pictures.

Picture Suggestions

apples	jam	quince
beans	kettle	ribbon
carrots	lace	salt
duck	maple	tea
eggs	syrup	umbrella
flour	nuts	vegetables
grapes	oats	wagon
hammer	pickles	yarn
ice		zinnias

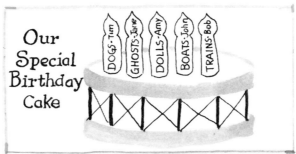

OUR SPECIAL BIRTHDAY CAKE

Decorate the bulletin board to look like a drum-shaped birthday cake (see illustration).

On the ditto machine, run off construction paper sheets filled with many burning birthday candle designs. (Each candle should be wide enough for a parent to write a book title and a child's name on it.) Send the candle sheets home with an explanation to parents that says each time a child reads a book, or has a book read to him, a candle should be filled out with the book's title and child's name. The child should cut out the candle, bring it to school, and put it on the cake. The more the children read, the more candles there will be on the cake. Encourage them to fill it up.

Explain to the children that the special cake is to celebrate the birthdays of Lincoln and Washington.

Lincoln liked to read so much that he often read by the light of a candle or the fireplace. General Washington also was a reader. Most great leaders are readers.

LEARNING
CENTERS

Lemon
Juice   Milk

INVISIBLE VALENTINES

You will need to provide sheets of white paper, small paint brushes or cotton swabs, scissors, a small bowl of lemon juice or milk, and a lamp with an unshaded bulb.

Everyone likes surprise messages. So children will enjoy visiting the "Invisible Valentine Message Center" to make valentines. Explain the procedure to the class as a whole, but let children go to the center one at a time. Be sure to have the instructions clearly posted in the center so children can work independently, following the step-by-step procedure. If using this with kindergarten children, an aide should stay in the Learning Center.

STEP ONE: Cut a heart shape from a piece of white paper. Think of a cute message to print on the heart.

STEP TWO: Dip a brush or cotton swab into lemon juice or milk. Print the message on the valentine. (Young children may draw pictures on the heart shapes.)

STEP THREE: Hang up the heart to dry. (If the message is quite wet to start, it will develop easier after it's dry.)

When all the children have had an opportunity to make a heart, and all the messages are dry, distribute them at random.

STEP FOUR: To make the message appear, hold the heart near a hot light bulb. (To avoid children burning themselves, teachers may want to demonstrate this before allowing children to come to this learning center. The writing will turn brown from the heat, allowing readability.)

VALENTINES ACROSS
THE MILES

This learning center is easy to set up, takes a relatively small amount of space, and helps develop children's sequencing abilities.

Make a series of simple sequence cards to show the steps a valentine takes when it is sent to someone who lives miles away. You may want to mount actual pictures on construction paper, or make your own simple sketches on paper. (The illustration here will guide you as you make your own simple pic-

ture cards. Also see Talk-About Time on page 15 for related ideas.)

On the backs of the cards, number them in the correct sequence so students can check themselves.

Allow students to visit the center independently, arrange the cards into sequence, turn the cards over to check the sequence, then mix up the cards again for the next student.

You may want to print what action the card shows next to the sequence number on the back.

PHONICS FUN WITH HEARTS

All you need to construct this learning center is a blank area on a wall, some cardboard, string, and magazine pictures.

Space out the letters in V-a-l-e-n-t-i-n-e across a piece of sturdy cardboard that is about three feet long and four inches wide. Attach a shoestring to the base of each letter. Make some cutout hearts. Mount pictures of objects that begin with each of the letters (for the "v," you might have pictures of a vase, violin, violets, and so on, each on a separate heart). Punch a hole, or holes, in each heart. Have the children take turns stringing each picture to the correct shoelace—the one attached to the letter that represents the beginning sound of the illustrated object. (To make the activity self-correcting, make the holes for each letter sound in the same position on the hearts; then, when the deck of responses is stacked, a picture strung incorrectly will be immediately apparent.)

by Annetta Dellinger

CHERRY COUNTING

This learning center idea can test and enhance your students' counting and association skills.

Cover 10 juice cans with white paper. Decorate each can with a different number of small red cherries made from construction paper. You should have one can for each number 1-10. Affix a picture hook to each can. Make blue number cards, 1-10, each with a hole punched at the top. Also provide red marbles or cardboard cherries.

Children may visit the center independently, or in pairs, and try to put the same number of cherries in a can as there are cherries decorating the outside. Once the child has put the correct number of cherries in a can, he hangs the appropriate number card on that can's picture hook. In this way, one-to-one correspondence, numerical sequencing, and counting skills are reinforced.

by Annetta Dellinger

OUR FAMOUS PRESIDENTS

When history is made close-up and personal, children are interested in learning more about it. Here is a learning-center idea that can help children feel the aspirations of courageous characters who have influenced history.

Obtain several simple picture and storybooks about the lives of George Washington and Abraham Lincoln. (Your local library should have several titles.)

If you teach second or third grade, create a cozy reading corner in your room where you can put up pictures of George Washington and

Abraham Lincoln, and attractively display the history books. Provide comfortable seating, some paper and pencils.

As children visit the center, they should decide to study about either Lincoln or Washington, read about the life of that person, and then write a limerick, poem, or letter to the rest of the class telling about that person's life — or an incident in the person's life.

After children have had an opportunity to visit the center, read the letters or poems aloud and/or post them for all to read.

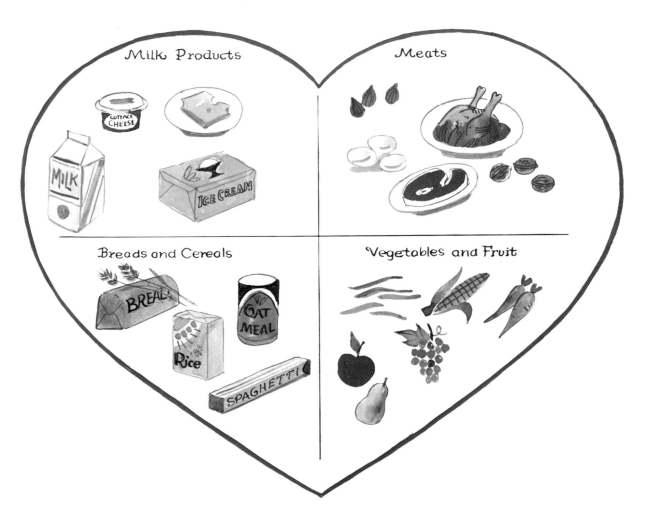

AMERICAN HEART MONTH — FEBRUARY

Valentine's Day is a day of the "heart." It can provide an opportunity to talk about things we can do to keep our hearts healthy — eat right, exercise, etc.

Find an area in your room where you can put a large heart shape and section it off into four parts. (See illustration.) Give each section a label: Milk Products; Meats; Breads and Cereals; Vegetables and Fruit. Below the heart poster, place a small table with magazine pictures, scissors, paste. Allow students to come to the learning center individually during the month, to find and paste up pictures of foods in the proper food groups.

COIN AND RIDDLE LEARNING CENTER

Abraham Lincoln, George Washington, and Susan B. Anthony all have birthdays in February. To get students thinking about the contributions of these famous individuals, set up a learning center where students can come individually for the following fun-to-do learning activities.

Riddle Me a Riddle

To set up a riddle area where children can come and work quietly, all you need is a desk or table, some lined paper, contact paper, tissues, and crayons.

Print out the three riddles below on lined paper. Leave a blank space at the bottom of each poem for a child to write in the answer to the riddle. (If you teach kindergarten, perhaps an aide could help in the Learning Center.) Use clear contact paper to laminate the riddle sheets so that they can be used by every child. Provide a crayon for the child to use to print the answer to each riddle. Have the answer printed upside down on the back of each riddle sheet so the child can check the answers. Provide tissues so each child can erase the answers before leaving.

Riddles

To help us remember our President,
They put his face on a penny.
Who was that famous leader of ours
Who was loved through the years
By so many?

_____

(Ans: *Abraham Lincoln*)

You can take a quarter,
And play a video game.
My picture's on the quarter.
Now tell me, what's my name?

_____

(Ans: *George Washington*)

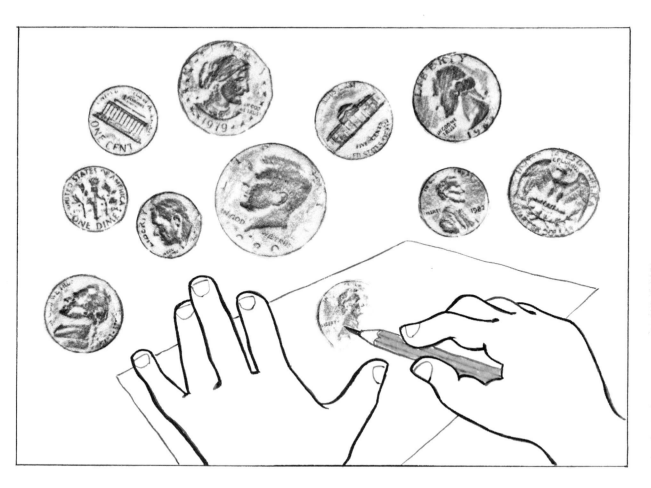

I did a lot for women.
　　That's how it came to be.
They put my face upon a coin,
　　Then named the coin for me.
Who am I?

_____

(Ans: *Susan B. Anthony*)

Make Coin Rubbings

For this section of the coin learning center, you'll need to provide pencils, sheets of manila paper, scissors, a penny, quarter, and if possible, a Susan B. Anthony silver dollar.

Before allowing children to come to this activity, demonstrate the steps involved. Also clearly list the steps at the center so older children can work successfully without help.

STEP ONE: Place a sheet of paper over a coin.

STEP TWO: Hold the paper with one hand to keep it from moving. Move your pencil lead back and forth over the coin. A picture will appear on your paper!

STEP THREE: Make enough coin rubbings so that you can cut them out, arrange them in sets, and practice counting.

by Dotti Hannum

STORIES ON TAPE

Because children love to be read to, tape-record some favorite valentine stories or interesting stories about Abe Lincoln or George Washington.

Then set up a center in your room where pupils may go individually and listen to the stories. (Be sure to provide earphones so students involved in other things won't be disturbed.)

Beforehand, instruct the children to draw pictures to illustrate the stories they hear. Each person should write a caption for his picture.

Display the pictures.

SUSAN B. ANTHONY DAY

February 15 is the birthday of Susan B. Anthony. We remember her for her efforts as an advocate of women's rights. In fact, Miss Anthony was one of the first women to vote.

Obtain some information on this courageous woman, and if you teach second or third graders, set up a learning center that focuses on her life. Also provide a variety of craft materials that children can use without help.

Have children visit the center individually, read the material, and then construct scenes that depict important events from the life of Susan B. Anthony. For example, a second-grade student might make a scene out of modeling clay and paper scraps showing Miss Anthony at a voting booth. (See illustration.)

"MY FAVORITE THINGS"

In celebration of Valentine's Day, allow your pupils an opportunity to share about what they love most.

Set up a learning center where children may go, one at a time, to paint pictures of their favorite activities or most treasured objects.

You'll need a small table covered with newspapers, tempera paint, painting smocks, brushes, juice cans of clear water, and paper.

(You may want to cut out large heart shapes from white construction paper. Let the children use them for their pictures.)

When everyone has had an opportunity to visit the learning center, and the paint has dried, let children tell the class what they've painted and why. Then hang up the heart-shaped pictures for special valentine decorations.

THINGS
TO MAKE
AND DO

GRAB AN IDEA

by Annetta Dellinger and Beth Holzbauer

MATCH THE VALENTINES: Draw various colors and sizes of valentines on a large sheet of poster paper. Cut out identical hearts from construction paper. Laminate the cut outs. Ask the children to match the hearts.

CLOTHESPIN CLIP: Obtain colored clothespins. On a strip of cardboard or wood, draw hearts with colored permanent markers which match your clothespin colors. Let the children match the colors by clipping the clothespins on the hearts.

VALENTINE WALK: Draw various colors of hearts on the backs of carpet squares. Put the squares on the floor in a circle. Let the children walk around the circle to music, stepping on the squares, until music stops. Without the children looking, take away one square. Then ask them to tell you what color is missing.

VALENTINE FIND: Hide various colors of valentines around the room. Pin or tape a different-colored heart on each child. Ask the children to walk around the room and find all the hearts that are the colors of the ones they are wearing.

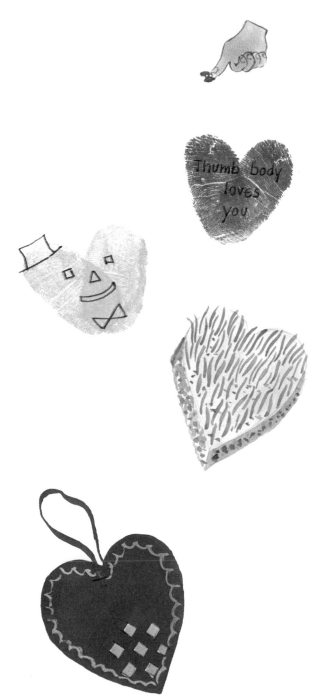

THUMBPRINT VALENTINES: Let each child make two thumbprints into a heart (see illustration). He may turn it into a character by adding features. Let him add the caption: "Thumb body loves you." You will need to provide paper and paints for this activity.

VALENTINE PLANT: Cut a sponge in the shape of a heart for each person. Let each child sprinkle rye-grass seed on his sponge. Keep the sponges wet. Watch the grass grow. The grass may need to be mowed with scissors so that it won't get too tall.

WEAVE A HEART: Cut hearts out of construction paper. At bottom of each heart cut 14 slits (see illustration). Cut strips, the width of the slits, out of paper in contrasting colors.

Let each pupil weave some strips through the slits on a heart. He should cut off the excess ends and tape the strips to the back of the heart. The student may staple a loop of curling ribbon to the top of the heart. Make a small bow and glue it to the heart (covering the staple). If desired, the child may write a valentine message on the heart.

VALENTINES FOR PARENTS

MINI-VALENTINE VASE

Provide red wooden macrame beads, small dried flowers, silk flowers, white tape, red craft ribbon, and wire.

To make: Take a piece of craft wire and shape it into a small heart. Twist one end of the wire around, leaving a 2-inch stem (see sketch). Glue the wire heart onto red craft ribbon. Cut out around it. Let it dry overnight.

Make a small flower arrangement in the macrame bead vase using the dried and silk flowers. Stick the ribbon heart into the vase. Write a Valentine message on white tape and put it on the vase. (Note: It may also be necessary to put a piece of tape over the bottom end of the macrame bead to keep the flowers from coming out.)

by Beth Holzbauer

HANDPRINT VALENTINES

Use 12-by-18 inch red construction paper, white tempera in a pie tin, and copies of poem.

POEM: *I'll use my hands to clean my room,*
And make the dishes shine,
To show my parents every day,
That I'm their valentine.

Fold a piece of red paper in half, lengthwise. One at a time, have each child spread his fingers wide, place his hand into the white paint, and make a handprint on the red paper. Blot well. Repeat, using the other hand (see sketch). Let the handprints dry overnight.

The next day, glue the poems to the insides of the cards (or the older children may print the poems themselves). Older children could also print "Hands Full of Love" on the front of the cards, and sign their names.

by Dotti Hannum

HATS TO MAKE AND WEAR

A HAT FOR GEORGE

Provide black, red, white, and blue construction paper, scissors, staples, and glue.

If you place the pattern here on a folded piece of paper and cut it double, you will make a pattern for the front of the hat. Let each person cut two hat pieces — front and back.

Staple each hat together at the sides so it fits the child's head.

Each person may cut red, white, and blue feathers from construction paper. Make each feather smaller than the one before. Staple the feathers — one on top of the other — to the front of the hat.

(Also see page 78 for a Lincoln hat.)

THREE-CORNERED HAT

Provide large, black, paper circles, or paper plates and black paint, scissors, staples, and stapler. Children may paint the paper plates black.

Fold the edges of the hat up as in the illustration. Staple the corners. Cut out the center section to fit a child's head.

Let each person put some feathers on his hat for decorations.

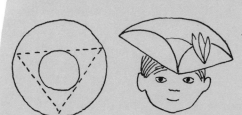

three-cornered hat

Pattern for Hat for George

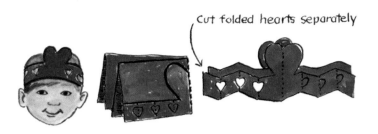

Cut folded hearts separately

KING AND QUEEN OF HEARTS CROWNS

Children will need red construction paper, scissors, and staples or tape.

To make: Have each child fold a sheet of construction paper in half lengthwise. Then fold it in half the opposite way (see sketch).

Cut a heart from the top to about 3/4 of the way down the fold, but do not cut it completely out at the point.

Cut from the outside across to the heart, up about 2 inches from the bottom, to make a headband.

Older students may want to cut out small hearts along the band to make the heart crowns more decorative. Let them do that. Then staple the two pieces of each crown together to form the hat.

BETSY ROSS BONNET

For each bonnet you will need fabric, and yarn or ribbon. Have large needles available.

Betsy's hat is made from a circle (10 or 12 inches in diameter) cut from cloth. If you have a room mother to help, you may want to hem the circles before continuing. Also let the room mother help each student use a needle and yarn or ribbon to sew a running-stitch around the circle. The stitch should be about one or two inches in from the edge, depending on how large a ruffle you want the cap to have.

Place the cap on the child's head and gather until it fits. Tie the yarn to keep the size. Cut off excess yarn or ribbon.

SOMETHING TO TRY

CREATE A STAMP

Give each child a 5-by-6-inch piece of construction paper, scissors, and markers, crayons, or paints.

Encourage each person to design a stamp by cutting scallops on the edges of his square with scissors and then creating a picture.

Perhaps you will want to show and talk about stamps from the U.S. Postal Service before you do this. Tie this in with mailing valentines.

PAPER WINDMILL

Provide 6-inch squares of paper, scissors, pencils with erasers (or plastic straws), and straight pins.

To make: Have each child fold the square paper in half diagonally to find the lines where he should cut. Then he should open it up and fold it the other direction (also on the diagonal).

Cut each of the fold lines from the corner almost to the center.

Fold one cut corner of each triangle into the center (see illustration). Put the pin through the center being sure to catch the four corners. Insert pin in eraser or through the straw. (If you use a straw, put a lump of play clay over the point on the pin.)

Adjust the paper so that it is loose enough to move when a breeze hits the blades. Use this project with a study of weather on Groundhog Day.

QUEEN OF HEARTS PARTY

The Queen of Hearts
She made some tarts,
All on a summer's day;
The Knave of Hearts
He stole the tarts,
And took them all away.

The King of Hearts
Called for the tarts,
And beat the knave full sore;
The Knave of Hearts
Brought back the tarts,
And vowed he'd steal no more.

GAMES

QUEEN OF HEARTS: Arrange chairs for players in a circle. (One chair per player.) Fasten a large paper heart behind one of the chairs. This is the Queen of Hearts' throne. To play, the players walk around the circle. At a prearranged signal, they try to find a chair. The person who sits in the chair with the heart on it must drop out of the game. Each time a player is eliminated, a chair is removed from the circle. The game ends when only one player is left.

HUNT THE HEARTS: Cut assorted hearts from paper and hide them in the room. Let the children hunt for them for a given period of time, then they may count the ones they find.

RUNNING KNAVES: Divide the class into two teams. Place large paper hearts at intervals on the floor in front of each team. The first player of each team will run to the other end of the room and back, stepping on each heart as he runs. When the first player returns to his line, the second player will run, and so on. The first team finished wins.

PASS THE VALENTINE: Use a small heart cut from construction paper or tag board as the marker. Play the game as you would "Who Has the Thimble?" Choose one person to be "it" in the center of the circle. "It" (with hands together, fingers up) goes to each player. He inserts the tips of his fingers into every player's hands. "It" drops the valentine into the hands of one player in the circle. He calls on someone to guess who has the valentine. If the person guesses, he becomes "it." A variation — the boys and girls pass the valentine around while singing, and when the music stops, the person inside the circle, who is "it," must guess who has the valentine. (See song on page 48.)

Valentine, Valentine

H.B.

Helen Bauman

Val - en-tine, Val - en-tine, Who has the Val - en - tine?

Pass it 'round the cir - cle, oh, so fine.

Is it me? Or is it you?

When the song is o - ver, then __ guess who!

DECORATIONS

ROYAL VALENTINE STRAWS: Materials you need are plastic straws and red plastic ribbon.

Cut two small hearts from the plastic ribbon. Cut two slits in each heart. Push the hearts onto the straw. Position them where they won't get into the drink or the child's mouth. Use the straws at your party.

by Beth Holzbauer

ROYAL CUPS: Provide white cold-drink cups and red heart-shaped stickers.

The children will enjoy decorating cups for the party.

Candy Basket

Placemat

Card Bag

THE QUEEN'S PLACEMATS: For each person provide one 12-by-18-inch sheet of white construction paper, one 9-by-12-inch sheet of red paper, red markers, scissors, and glue.

To make: Decorate the white paper by cutting and gluing on red hearts, or by drawing red valentines on it. Scallop the edges.

(Children may make their own placemats while the teacher and helping mother are setting up the party table with treats or ice cream sundaes.)

by Dotti Hannum

THE KING'S CANDY BASKET: Red construction paper, lace doilies, colorful stickers, and glue.

To make: Cut two identical hearts and a strip of paper (about 3/4-by-6-inches) from red construction paper. Glue small round doilies to the two hearts.

Fold hearts in half. Put the points of the hearts together with one heart inside of the other (see illustration). Glue the overlapping areas together. But be careful not to smear the glue inside. Decorate with stickers.

Glue the handle at the top as illustrated. When it's dry, fill the basket with candy hearts and nuts.

KNAVE'S VALENTINE CARD BAG: Obtain red construction paper, curling ribbon, and chalk, markers, or crayons.

To make: Cut two large hearts (approximately 12-by-11-inches each).

Staple the hearts together along the outside edges and point, but not around the tops. Or punch holes and lace them together. Tie two bows with the curling ribbon. Staple one to each side of the heart-shaped bag. Decorate the bag however you want. (If the children put their names on the hearts, they can put their valentines inside.)

by Beth Holzbauer

REFRESHMENTS

Red Heart Cake

Let the children mix up a package of their favorite cake mix and bake it, according to the directions, in two pans—one a nine-inch square pan, the other a nine-inch round pan.

When the cakes are baked and properly cooled, an aide may cut the round cake in equal halves. Place the halves of the round cake against adjoining sides of the square cake (as in the illustration) to form a heart. Let some children decorate the cake heart with red frosting and any special decorations they choose.

King's Choice Punch

Strawberry or cherry
  powdered drink mix

Lemon-lime soda
Heart-shaped ice cubes

Ahead of time, freeze some red heart-shaped ice cubes in jello molds. Combine the ingredients in a punch bowl; mix; and serve it from the refreshment table.

Queen of Hearts Tarts

Before time for the party, you will want to ask if the children understand what the Queen of Hearts made when she made some tarts. If they don't, talk about tarts before you make them for the party.

1 cup flour
1/3 cup plus
   1 tablespoon shortening

2 tablespoons water
Pinch of salt

Cream the flour and shortening together. Add the water and salt, and mix well. Roll into small balls, just like play dough. Press balls down into muffin tins with your thumb. Flute. Bake 8 to 10 minutes at 350 degrees. Cool, and fill with raspberry, strawberry, or cherry preserves, or pie filling. Add a squirt of canned whipped cream to the top of each one.

by Annetta Dellinger

Queen of Hearts Sundaes

Have a room mother scoop the ice-cream balls ahead of time. Keep them in a large container in the freezer. (Have the children bring the various toppings.)

Assorted ice-cream toppings:

chocolate
butterscotch
chopped nuts
whipped cream

cherries
strawberries
sliced bananas
raisins

Call two or three children at a time. Let them make their own sundaes from the QUEEN'S SUNDAE TABLE (set up with the ice-cream balls and toppings).

by Dotti Hannum

SPECIAL TREATS FOR OTHER FEBRUARY HOLIDAYS

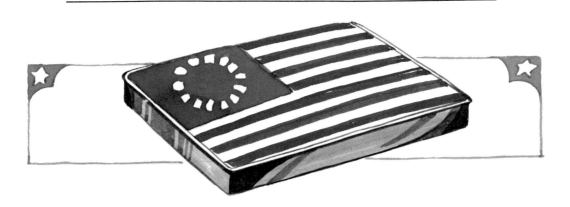

BETSY ROSS FLAG CAKE

After you talk about Betsy Ross and the first flag, let the children make a colonial flag cake using the recipe below.

2 cups flour
1²/₃ cups sugar
1¼ tsp. baking soda
¼ tsp. baking powder
²/₃ cup cocoa
1¹/₃ cups water
1 cup mayonnaise

3 eggs
1 tsp. vanilla
1 can white cake frosting
Blue food coloring
13 miniature marshmallows
7 strips of cherry licorice
13-by-9-by-2-inch baking dish or pan

In advance, set oven at 350°. Grease and flour the pan. Then mix flour, sugar, baking soda, and baking powder together in a big bowl. Sift in cocoa.

Add water, mayonnaise, eggs, and vanilla to the mixture. Mix well with fork. Bake 40 minutes, or until a toothpick stuck in the center comes out clean. Let cake cool.

Let an aide help students decorate cake. Put ½ cup of the frosting into a small bowl. Add a few drops of the blue food coloring, and stir it into the frosting. Continue adding food coloring until frosting is a medium blue.

Spread the white frosting on the cooled cake.

Spread the blue frosting in the left top corner of the cake.

Lay out the red licorice in seven even rows, starting from the top, to make the red stripes on the cake. You may cut the licorice into pieces to do this.

Use the marshmallows for stars on the blue square.

by Dotti Hannum

LINCOLN-LOG CAKE

1 cup flour
1 tsp. baking powder
1/4 tsp. salt
1/4 cup cocoa
3 eggs

1 cup sugar
1/3 cup water
1 tsp. vanilla
Confectioner's sugar

To celebrate Lincoln's birthday, an aide may help students make this cake. Blend flour, baking powder, salt, and cocoa. Beat eggs, and mix in. Gradually beat in the sugar, water, and vanilla.

Pour batter into greased jelly-roll pan. (The cake will come out more easily if you line the bottom of the pan with aluminum foil or greased brown paper.) Bake 12-15 minutes at 350 degrees. Remove from oven.

Loosen edges, and turn the cake upside down on a kitchen towel. Remove the paper. Sprinkle with confectioner's sugar.

While the cake is hot, roll up the cake and towel from the narrow end.

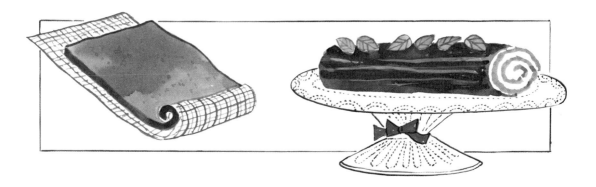

When cool, unroll the cake. Remove the towel. Spread the cake with whipped cream or non-dairy topping. Roll up the cake carefully.

Let pupils frost the cake with chocolate icing. Run the point of a knife lengthwise in the frosting to make it look like bark. You can decorate the "log" with green, spearmint, leaf-shaped gumdrops. Chill thoroughly.

by Ruth Shannon Odor

WASHINGTON'S CHERRY TREE COOKIES

⅔ cup butter or margarine   1⅔ cup flour
⅓ cup sugar   red, green, and brown
½ tsp. almond extract   food coloring

Let an aide help pupils—a few at a time—work on this.

In a large bowl, cream butter and sugar until fluffy. Add almond extract. Gradually add flour, beating slowly until well blended.

Divide mixture into three parts. Drop a few drops of red food coloring into one part of the dough. Knead the dough with your hands until the color is well mixed and the dough is smooth. Repeat with green and brown food colorings. (Instead of using brown food coloring, you may choose to leave that part of the dough its natural color.)

Form tree trunks out of the brown dough, treetops out of the green dough, and cherries on the tree out of the red dough.

Place the cookie trees about one-inch apart on ungreased cookie sheets and bake at 300° for 20 to 25 minutes (or until edges are firm, but not brown). Lift cookies with a spatula, and place on waxed paper to cool.

by Dotti Hannum

GEORGE WASHINGTON TREAT

A legend says that when he was a little boy, George Washington chopped down his father's favorite cherry tree. When his father asked him if he did it, George told the truth.

To make a cherry treat, you will need vanilla ice cream (one scoop per child), two cans of cherry pie filling, pan and heat source, electric fry pan or wok, 1 bowl per child, and 1 spoon per child. Let an aide help with this.

Pour the cherry pie filling into the pan. Heat it over low heat, stirring constantly, until filling is hot.

Scoop a dipper of ice cream into each bowl. Pour two big spoonfuls of cherry pie filling over each dip. Enjoy!

by Dotti Hannum

GAMES AND RHYTHMIC ACTIVITIES

CHILDREN ON PARADE

FIFE AND DRUM BAND

On pages 43 and 44 are directions for making colonial hats. Let the students make the hats, and then pretend to be a fife and drum marching band. Provide toy drums and whistles for the children to play as they march.

FLAG PARADE

To have a flag parade, the children will need flags to carry. See page 22 for a suggestion of how to make a flag. When each person has finished his flag, have a parade carrying the flags. Play marching music such as a Sousa march.

ACTION RHYMES

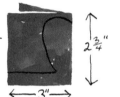

THE VALENTINE TREE

(Besides holding up fingers for each number, let students ad lib other movements. By the last stanza, students should be holding up all 10 fingers. The hands will disappear behind their backs as they finish. Children may also make and wear finger puppets, as illustrated.)

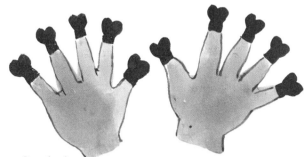

Grandma sends a valentine,
  Especially for you.
You find another.
  Then you have two.

Two little valentines.
  You hang them on a tree.
Mom adds another one;
  Now there are three.

Three little valentines.
  But still there's room for more.
Dad brings another one.
  Then you have four.

Four little valentines.
  Will more arrive?
Here comes Aunt Mary's.
  Now there are five.

Five little valentines.
  Here's one that ticks.
Still you hang it on the tree;
  That gives you six.

Six little valentines.
  And here comes Kevin.
He brings another one.
  Now you have seven.

Seven little valentines.
  The carrier brings one late.
You add it to the tree.
  So now there are eight.

Eight little valentines.
  You go out to dine.
You get another one.
  Now you have nine.

Nine little valentines.
  "One more," says Uncle Ben.
He hangs it on your tree.
  Now you have ten.

Ten little valentines,
  All in a row.
Here comes a mighty wind,
  And there they go!

CHORES

Abe Lincoln chopped a tree one
    day.
    (Pretend to chop down a tree.)
He split it into rails.
    (Pretend to split logs.)
He stacked them up beside the
    house,
    (Stack lumber.)
Between the water pails.
    (Make circle with hands.)

BEING VALENTINES

*(Let students make large red or
white hearts to wear.)*

"Let's be valentines," Sarah said.
"You be white and I'll be red."
Each one made a giant heart,
And put it on to act the part.

"The only thing," asked Harold
    Drew,
"Is what's a valentine to do?"
    *(Stop here and let the children
    suggest actions. Do them, or use
    the rest of the poem for actions.)*
"Let's bow and skip and run; now
    stop,
And spin around like a valentine
    top."

GAMES GALORE

HONEST ABE

Explain that for awhile Abraham Lincoln worked in a grocery store. One day he charged a woman six and one-fourth cents too much for what she bought. That night, after the store was closed, Abe walked three miles to her house and gave the money back to the woman. That's probably why he had the nickname, "Honest Abe."

Play this game based on the story. Divide into two teams. Choose a person from each team to be the customer. Seat the customers at one end of the room facing the teams. On a table to the side of each team, place a bowl of pennies. Players, in turn, must count out seven pennies, go pay their customers, and return, to let the next players pay their debts. The first team to get finished wins.

WALK THE LOG

Lumberjacks like to walk on logs. Sometimes they do it in pairs on a log that is floating. They try to get the log spinning so one of them falls off. Being around trees and in the woods, Abe Lincoln surely tested his skill and balance by walking on logs.

Provide two planks or logs. Divide the group into teams for a log-walking relay. Each player will walk down the log, run back, tag the next teammate in line, and go to the end of the line. The first team finished wins. A player who slips off the log must go back and try again. You may want to do this outside.

ALPHABET HEARTS

Place several dozen small paper or cardboard hearts with alphabet letters on them in a box. Shake them up. Seat players in a circle formation. "It" should take one heart from the box, and call out the letter on it. The first player to raise his hand and say a word which begins with that letter wins the heart. And he gets to call out the next letter. The player who gets the most hearts wins the game.

CUPID CHASE

Blindfold all players except one. He will be "Cupid." Tie a small bell around his neck. "Cupid" may move around the area as he wishes. The blindfolded players try to catch "Cupid" by listening for his bell. When a player tags him, the two should exchange places.

CHOP THE CHERRY TREE

All but three players will scatter themselves around the playing area. They become the "cherry trees." They are rooted in place and may only squat or stand up. The three players left will be "hatchets." The trees stand — unless a hatchet approaches — then they may squat. If a hatchet sneaks up and touches a tree while it is standing, that tree is considered chopped down, and the player must sit on the floor. The trees may squat whenever a hatchet is approaching, but they must get up as soon as the hatchet passes. A tree is "chopped" if it remains down or squats when a hatchet is not approaching.

POEMS
AND
SONGS

(On Groundhog Day, why not read the following poem to your class? Let them act out the poem as you read it.)

MY SHADOW

I have a little shadow that goes in
　　and out with me,
And what can be the use of him is
　　more than I can see.
He is very, very like me from the
　　heels up to the head;
And I see him jump before me,
　　when I jump into my bed.

The funniest thing about him is the
　　way he likes to grow—
Not at all like proper children,
　　which is always very slow;
For he sometimes shoots up taller
　　like an India-rubber ball,
And he sometimes gets so little that
　　there's none of him at all.

He hasn't got a notion of how
　　children ought to play,
And can only make a fool of me in
　　every sort of way.
He stays so close beside me, he's a
　　coward you can see;
I'd think shame to stick to mommie
　　as that shadow sticks to me!

One morning, very early, before
　　the sun was up,
I rose and found the shining dew on
　　every buttercup;
But my lazy little shadow, like an
　　arrant sleepyhead,
Had stayed at home behind me and
　　was fast asleep in bed.
　　　　by Robert Louis Stevenson

VALENTINE FUN

A valentine is fun to send.
I took one to my next-door
    friend.
I made it myself with hearts
    and lace—
And wrote a special line.
I wrote it BIG. Here's what
It said: BE MY VALENTINE!
                    by Jane Buerger

MY VALENTINE COOKIES

Mother made some cookies.
    I put them on my tray.
And since today is special,
    I'm giving them away.
                    by Kay Wilson

DO YOU LOVE ME?

Do you love me or do you not?
You told me once but I forgot.
                    Anonymous

ON VALENTINE'S DAY
AND EVERY DAY

Love the beautiful,
    Seek out the true,
Wish for the good,
    And the best do!
                    by Felix Mendelssohn

BIG, BIGGER, BIGGEST

Penelope, Sharon, and Wanda
   May
Each made snowballs one winter
   day.
"Mine is biggest," said Penelope.
Sharon and Wanda turned to see.
"Sharon's is bigger than yours is
   too.
"I have an idea for what we can
   do."
Penelope, Sharon, and Wanda
   May
Stacked up their snowballs that
   winter day.
I'm sure by now you're about to
   guess,
They made a snowman in winter
   dress.
Said Sharon, "I'll give him a heart
   of mine,
"And we can call him our valentine."
by Sandi Veranos

MY VALENTINE

Wouldn't it be funny?
   Wouldn't it be fine?
If only I could get Jack Frost,
   To be my valentine?

He'd draw upon my window,
   With his crystal frost and brush,
And write among the lazy hearts,
   "I love you very much."
by Kay Wilson

MY QUARTERS

I had a stack of quarters
   With Washington on each one.
I spent them playing Pac-Man
   And had a lot of fun.
by Sandi Veranos

64

PUZZLES

Do you think an alarm
   Rings under the ground
To tell the groundhog
   To look around?

How does he know
   When it's the right day
To look out and tell us
   Spring's on its way?

by Kay Wilson

ON WASHINGTON'S
BIRTHDAY

Father took us shopping.
   We got new shoes to wear.
Since it was Washington's birthday,
   There were sales everywhere.
We stopped in at a restaurant
   And ordered cherry pie.
And all sang, "Happy Birthday,
   George,"
   Jackie, Jane, and I.

by Kay Wilson

MR. LINCOLN'S LETTER

The carrier knocked upon the door.
   Abe Lincoln called, "Come in,"
And reached to get a letter—
   He knew it was for him.

When he ripped it open,
   Imagine his delight
To find he had a valentine
   That was lacy, red, and white.

Said Lincoln, with a chuckle,
   "I think it's mighty fine
That I can be both President
   And someone's Valentine."
              by Sandra Ziegler

BETSY'S NEEDLE

"Betsy, get your needle.
    Betsy, bring your thread.
Make our country's flag for us.
    Blue and white and red."

"Do you want a big one?
    Or should the flag be small?
What should be the shape of it?
    A square? A box? A ball?"

"Betsy, here's a picture
    I brought for you to see.
I drew it on some paper.
    Come! Look at it with me."

"I think it's very nice, sir,
    The red, the white, the blue.
If every star has five points,
    Is that all right with you?"

"I think that would be perfect,"
    Said General George aloud.
"And when this flag is flying,
    Our nation will be proud."

So Betsy took her needle.
    She sewed with all her might.
She made our very first flag,
    Of red and blue and white.
                by Sandra Ziegler

67

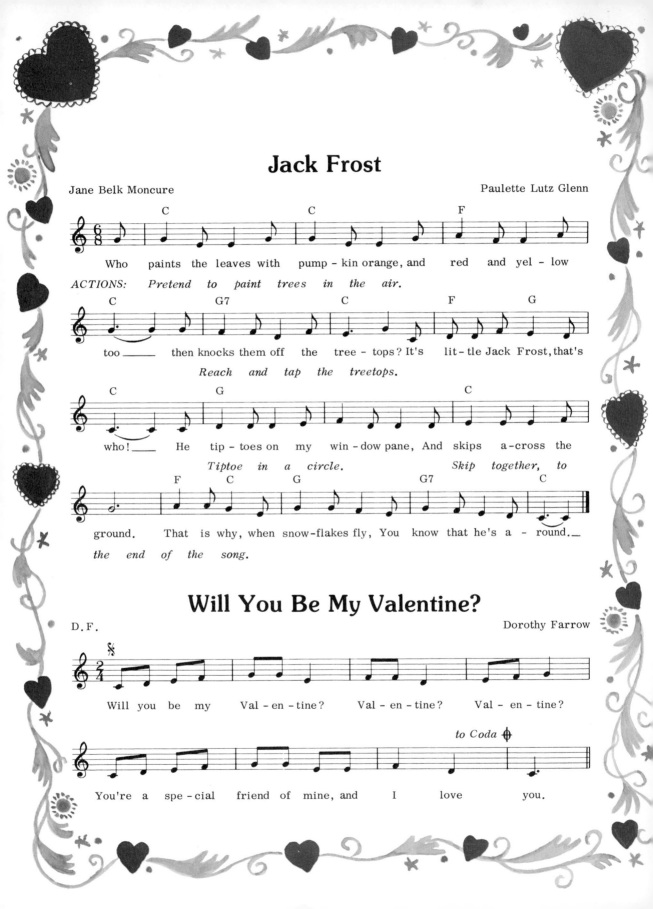

Jack Frost

Jane Belk Moncure

Paulette Lutz Glenn

Who paints the leaves with pump - kin orange, and red and yel - low

ACTIONS: Pretend   to   paint   trees   in   the   air.

too ____ then knocks them off the tree - tops? It's lit - tle Jack Frost, that's

Reach   and   tap   the   treetops.

who! ____ He tip - toes on my win - dow pane, And skips a - cross the

Tiptoe   in   a   circle.   Skip   together,   to

ground.   That is why, when snow-flakes fly, You know that he's a - round. ___

the   end   of   the   song.

Will You Be My Valentine?

D.F.

Dorothy Farrow

Will you be my Val - en - tine? Val - en - tine? Val - en - tine?

to Coda

You're a spe - cial friend of mine, and I love you.

I like it when you smile at me, or laugh and share a joke. It

D.S. al Coda

"pops" a smile in – side of me and makes me want to know_____

CODA

you. And I_____ love____ you!_____ Friends!

A Valentine Wish

Jane Belk Moncure

Jane Belk Moncure
Trans. by Paulette Lutz Glenn

If

1. I were the rain,____ Guess what I'd do?
2. I were a tree,____ Guess what I'd do?
3. I were a gar – den, Guess what I'd do?
4. I were the sky,____ Guess what I'd do?

REFRAIN

I would rain Val – en – tine rain-drops for you. You would
I would drop Val – en – tine leaves____ for you.
I would bloom Val – en – tine ros – es for you.
I would light Val – en – tine stars____ for you.

have e – nough Val – en – tines all through the year, to

Fine

D.C. al Fine

bring you my love and a bunch of good cheer! If

My Special Valentine

R.M.P.

Ruth Morgan Powell

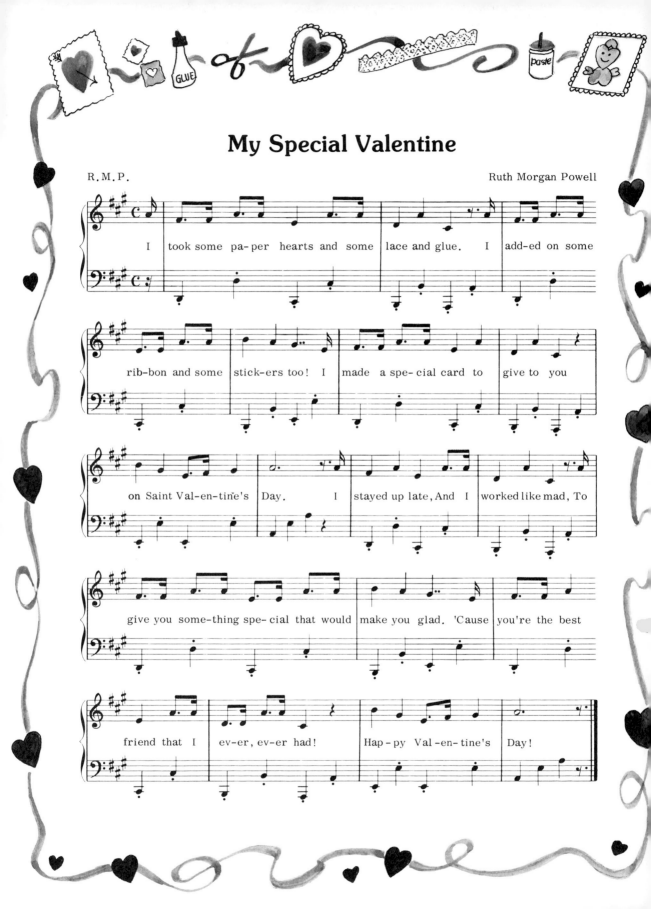

I took some pa-per hearts and some lace and glue. I add-ed on some

rib-bon and some stick-ers too! I made a spe-cial card to give to you

on Saint Val-en-tine's Day. I stayed up late, And I worked like mad, To

give you some-thing spe-cial that would make you glad. 'Cause you're the best

friend that I ev-er, ev-er had! Hap-py Val-en-tine's Day!

Piggy's Valentine

Two Great Presidents

R.M.P.

Ruth Morgan Powell

1. Two great pres-i-dents, Wash-ing-ton and Lin-coln, Lead-ers of a na-tion, both great and strong. Two great pres-i-dents once were chil-dren, learn-ing, grow-ing, all day long. 2. I could be a pres-i-dent like Wash-ing-ton or Lin-coln, Liv-ing in A-mer-i-ca, the land that's free. Then some day, a hun-dred years from now, kids could go to school and learn a song a-bout me!

BACKGROUND AND ACTIVITIES

GROUNDHOG DAY

by Ruth Shannon Odor

February 2 traditionally is known as Groundhog Day. Have you ever seen a groundhog? Sometimes a groundhog is called a woodchuck.

Some animals make homes in holes under the ground. There they sleep all winter long. Long ago, medieval folk thought that these animals came out of their burrows, every February 2, to take a look around and check on the weather. But not all folks watched for the same animals to appear.

In some countries, the animal they looked for was the hedgehog. In Germany they watched for the badger. Germans thought that if the sun shined, the badger would see his shadow. He would be frightened. He would crawl back inside his hole to sleep for six more weeks. Spring would come late.

To farmers this meant that they should look for more cold weather to come. Perhaps they should wait to plant their crops until later.

When the sky was cloudy and gray, the badger would not see his shadow. He would stay out of his burrow. Spring would come early.

People of England and Scotland said about the same thing in a weather rhyme:

"If Candlemas* be fair and bright,
Winter will have another flight;
But if it is dark with clouds and rain,
Winter is gone and will not come again."

*Candlemas was an important Christian holiday that the church celebrated with lighted candles on February 2.

The idea of a hibernating animal predicting weather was brought to America by early settlers from Germany. Since there were no badgers in the eastern part of the United States, the settlers chose the groundhog to be "the weather prophet."

Most of the German settlers made homes in what is now the state of Pennsylvania. Today Pennsylvania has several groundhog clubs that watch for appearances every February 2, and then they forecast the weather. They also argue with other clubs around the country about which groundhog is the true weather prophet.

Of course, the groundhog cannot really predict the weather. But it is fun to notice if February 2 is sunshiny, or cloudy, and then see if spring comes early or late.

ACTIVITIES

1. On February 2, talk about and record the weather. Figure out when the end of six weeks will be. Mark that day on the calendar. Each day make a note about the weather. See when spring comes.

2. Make a weather chart for the classroom. To do this, cut a circle from poster board. With a felt pen, divide the circle into five sections.

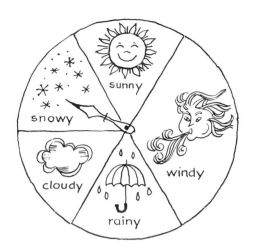

Print "sunny," "cloudy," "windy," "snowy," "rainy." Then draw a sketch to indicate the specific type of weather. Cut a little groundhog or arrow from construction paper. Fasten it to the chart with a paper fastener. Each day talk about the weather. Have someone move the pointer to that type of weather. You might also make pictures for "warm" and "cold," and place the proper one beside the chart.

3. Write and present a play about a groundhog coming out of the ground on Groundhog Day.

4. Visit a zoo, and see a real groundhog.

5. Take turns making shadow pictures on the wall. Use the poem on page 62.

ABRAHAM LINCOLN'S BIRTHDAY

by Ruth Shannon Odor

What do you think of when someone mentions Abraham Lincoln? A log cabin? Split rail fences? Books? Many symbols of Lincoln remind us of stories about him.

Abraham Lincoln was born in a cabin made of logs in Hardin County, Kentucky. The logs in his house had been split with an axe and fitted together at the corners. The holes and cracks, where they didn't match too well, were filled with clay mud. The Lincoln cabin was only one room, with one window, and one door. In winter an oiled deer hide was stretched across the window to keep out the cold air. A big fireplace, with crackling logs, provided heat, light, and a place for cooking meals.

If you visit Hodgenville, Kentucky, you can see that log cabin. It is on the Lincoln farm, which is now a national park known as the Abraham Lincoln Birthplace National Historical Site. Now the cabin is inside a large marble and granite building to protect it from the weather.

The Lincoln family moved from Kentucky to Indiana and then to Illinois. There they built another log cabin. Abe split rails to make a fence around the cabin and the ten acres of ground.

Abe was tall, lanky, and strong. He split lots and lots of fence rails. Once he split 1,000 rails for a neighbor. He used the money he earned to buy a pair of jeans. What a lot of work for a pair of jeans!

Abe Lincoln learned to read and write when he was six years old. He liked to read. Abe read the Bible. He walked miles to neighbors' houses to borrow books. He read the *Farmer's Almanac, Pilgrim's Progress, Aesop's Fables,* and he

read all about the life of George Washington.

Abe read, lying in front of the fireplace, with the flickering flames for light. He worked at learning arithmetic and writing too. He had no pencil and paper, not even a slate. He wrote and figured on the back of a wooden shovel with a charred stick.

Abe's mother died when he was a little boy. His stepmother wanted him to read and write. "Leave Abe alone. Let him read," she would say.

Abe slept in the loft of the log cabin. Sometimes he put the book he was reading in the crack in the roof to keep it safe. One night a storm came up. The rain beat against the cabin roof. Some water dripped down inside the loft. When

Abe woke up the next morning, he found his book soaking wet—and ruined! "What shall I do?" said Abe. He had borrowed the book from a rich farmer. The farmer was not very kind or understanding. He made Abe work for three days husking corn to pay for the ruined book.

Abe loved books so much that sometimes he read a book as he walked along between the handles of a plow.

In the town of New Salem, Abe Lincoln took care of a store. When there were no customers, he had time to read. In the winter he stretched his long legs out on the counter and read and read. In the summer he sat under a shade tree outside the store and read.

One day at the bottom of a barrel,

he found a thick book. It was a book about law. Lincoln began studying that book of law. He decided to become a lawyer. And the lawyer became a congressman. And the congressman became president of the United States!

ACTIVITIES

1. Obtain a copy of *Aesop's Fables*. Read a fable to the children.

2. (Use this activity as an individual or a class project.) Cover a table with green poster board or shelf paper. Build a miniature log cabin with *Lincoln Logs*. Put one door and one window in the cabin. Make a tabletop scene.

3. Show a collection of different kinds of hats. Talk about them. Show a picture of Lincoln wearing a stovepipe hat. Talk about when he was president and perhaps about his assassination.

4. Before class prepare a large stovepipe hat. To do this, cover a large tin can with black construction paper. Make a brim for the hat from posterboard, and glue it at the bottom of the can. Write some questions or true and false statements about Lincoln on slips of paper. Place these in the hat. Let the children take turns drawing questions and answering them.

5. Let each child make a stovepipe hat. Explain: make cuts about 1½-inches deep and 1-inch apart along a long side of a sheet of black construction paper. Make a circle with the paper, overlap the edges and fasten them together. Fold the flaps outward. Cut a brim. Paste or staple the flaps of the hat below the brim.

VALENTINE'S DAY

by Ruth Shannon Odor

(Write the word "valentine" on the chalkboard.) Once "valentine" was simply a word to mean "sweetheart." *(Write: "Be my valentine." "I will be your valentine.")* Gradually, down through the years, the meaning of the word changed. So today when we say "valentine," we usually mean a valentine card. Of course, when we say, "Be my valentine" on the card, we still use the word to mean sweetheart.

When the early settlers first came to America, they had little time to celebrate Valentine's Day. Gradually that changed. The first valentine cards they sent to each other were homemade.

A girl named Esther Howland began to make valentines. Hers became so popular and sold so well that soon she had a regular assembly line going, making valentines for others. She turned out many, many lovely valentines. Esther Howland's pretty valentines made Valentine's Day more popular in America.

In the early 1800's, factories began to make valentine cards. They printed black and white pictures on paper. Some of them were hand-painted by factory workers. Most people bought plain pictures and did the painting themselves. Some valentines had verses printed on them. Some were blank, and people wrote their own messages or copied messages from books.

After the post office began to sell stamps, people bought millions of valentines. They mailed them across the country.

As the custom of giving valentines grew, children began to have valentine parties. And grownups planned dinners and dances. People began to give heart-shaped candy, or jewelry, clothing, and other special gifts with their valentine wishes.

Today, valentines are still exchanged by both children and adults. And Valentine's Day is a happy holiday. People of all ages think of it as a time for telling others they are liked.

ACTIVITIES

1. Heart-shaped objects are everywhere on Valentine's Day. Can you think of some heart-shaped things you have seen? (Heart-shaped candies, candy boxes, pins, lockets, earrings, decorations for classrooms, and jello molds.)

The heart shape stands for feelings of love and friendship. Explain that to celebrate Valentine's Day, people often want to make red hearts. Show the children how to cut hearts from red construction paper. Use the hearts to decorate the room, make a heart mobile, or

outline the bulletin board. Or make a collage of hearts (outlined, cut out, colored, pin-pricked, etc).

2. Show some little pastel hard-candy hearts with mottoes on them. Explain that valentine mottoes have been around for many years. At first they were quite serious. Nowadays they are usually silly ones, such as "Me, too;" "Hey, you;" and "You bet." Can you think of some others? Give each child some candy hearts. Talk about the mottoes.

3. In Europe many years ago, groups of children went from house to house on Valentine's Day singing a good morning song like this:

"Good morning to you,
  Valentine:
Curl your locks as I do mine.
Two before, and three behind.
Good morning to you,
  Valentine."

Sometimes the people who lived in the houses came to the doors and gave the children apples, currant buns, or pennies.

Print the song on the chalkboard. Sing it together to a made-up tune.

4. Long before people sent valentine cards on Valentine's Day, they sent flowers. Flowers have always been connected with love and romance.

Let the children make flowers from construction paper. (See page 18.) Give the flowers as gifts.

5. Show a picture of Cupid. In ancient Rome, Cupid was said to be the son of Venus, the goddess of love. The Greeks called him Eros, the son of Aphrodite, their goddess of love.

Some said that Cupid shot a person in the heart with his arrow and made him or her fall in love. He was a natural to become a part of Valentine's Day lore. At first Cupid was pictured as a handsome young man, but now he is shown as a cute cherub. Pictures of Cupid are often used on valentine cards. The happy, chubby fellow will always be a part of Valentine's Day.

In class make a valentine box for the classroom. Use cutouts of Cupid, bows and arrows, and hearts to decorate it.

GEORGE WASHINGTON'S BIRTHDAY

by Ruth Shannon Odor

What is the first thing you think of when someone mentions George Washington's birthday? Was your answer cherries? Cherry pie?

Writers of history today tell us that the story of George and the cherry tree is probably not true. Whether the story is true or not, we do know that George Washington was a truthful person. And having cherry pie on his birthday is an UMMMM good idea!

When George Washington was eleven years old, his father died. George went to live with his older brother, Lawrence. Lawrence lived on a large beautiful plantation in Virginia. It was called Hunting Creek Farm. Lawrence named it Mount Vernon. " 'Mount' is for the high bank above the river," Lawrence told George. "And 'Vernon' is for my friend, Admiral Vernon." Later George became the owner of the plantation. But he did not change its name.

George married Martha Custis, a widow with two small children. They lived at Mount Vernon.

George Washington was the leader of the American army during the Revolutionary War.

One winter he and his army made camp at Valley Forge—a piece of land northwest of Philadelphia. It was named for an old iron furnace (called a forge) on Valley Creek Road.

When the army walked into the camp on December 19, 1777, the

soldiers were cold and hungry. Many were sick. Their clothes were tattered, and they had no shoes. Their bare feet left tracks of blood on the white snow.

The men who were building log huts for the soldiers to stay in built big bonfires. The tired soldiers lay down with their cold feet to the warm flames.

The winter at Valley Forge was long and cold. They had little food. Washington wrote letters, begging for supplies, but few supplies came.

Winter storms came. But not the enemy. For some reason the enemy general did not attack.

Although the men were cold and hungry, they became close friends. They all were fighting for freedom. They were proud of their general. He rode by on his horse on those cold winter days. If *he* believed enough in freedom to be there instead of in his warm, cozy home, then they did too!

After the war was over, George went back to his family at Mount Vernon. When George Washington was president, he lived in New York City and then Philadelphia. After that, he went back to his home at Mount Vernon.

You can visit Mount Vernon today. The house has been fixed up to look much the same as it did when Washington lived there.

ACTIVITIES

1. Make a display of money, including the dollar bill, with Washington's picture on it. Put the display where children may see it.

2. In class make an easy cherry "pie." You will need a can of orange Danish rolls and a can of cherry-pie filling for each pie. Have some children put the cherries in a pie pan or casserole dish. Let them pull the Danish rolls apart and put them over the cherries in a lattice design. Bake the pie in the oven at 350 degrees until the top is golden brown. Spread orange icing on top.

3. Mason Locke Weems, one of the men who first wrote about the life of George Washington, told many exciting stories besides the one about the cherry tree. One was about a silver dollar. He said Washington threw a silver dollar all the way across the Potomac River. That's a long way to throw a silver dollar, don't you think?

Let the children take turns trying to throw a silver dollar into a bowl several inches in front of them.

4. Make some room decorations using cherries and hatchets as the motif. (See patterns.)

5. Learn and sing a song George Washington might have sung, such as "Yankee Doodle" (emphasizing the third stanza) or "My Hat It Has Three Corners." Check at a library for a book of Revolutionary War songs to find words and music to use in the classroom.

Patterns

STORIES
TO READ
AND TELL

THE MYSTERY VALENTINE

by Beth Holzbauer

It was February. Jeff jumped off the bus and hurried right home. He did not take time to kick rocks or share funny stories with a friend. It was just too cold.

As Jeff hurried toward his warm home, he thought about the good kitchen smells of Mom's cooking. He quickened his steps—faster and faster. Something white was sticking out from his front door. Jeff stopped. What was it? It was an envelope. Jeff's name was on it.

Jeff took the envelope and went inside. He dropped his books and lunch box on a chair and ran to his room. What could it be? Who was it from?

Jeff opened the envelope. It was a valentine! The message read, "To someone special—I love you very much!" A dollar bill fell out of the card onto the floor. Jeff was glad to see it, but who was the card from? Jeff looked and looked, but no name was on the card.

"Mom," Jeff called, "do you know who gave me this card with the dollar in it? Is it from you?" He went to show her his valentine message, "To someone special—I love you very much!"

"I don't know who it is from," said Mother. "I never saw it before."

Jeff walked slowly back to his room. He sat down on his bed. "Hmmmm," he said. "I wonder if Dad gave it to me. He loves me. He takes me fishing and plays football with me.

"Maybe it really is from Mom.

She likes to do special things. Sometimes she puts football cards under my pillow for a surprise. I know she loves me; she tells me so all the time.

"No, I know! It's from Grandma and Grandpa. They're always wanting me to come to their house for a visit. They love me a lot too. And I love them. I have fun when I visit them.

"But it could be from my sister, Amy. Sure we fight. But deep down inside, I know she loves me. And I love her. Yesterday she shared her candy bar with me.

"Could it be from my teacher? She says nice things about my school work when I try real hard.

"It's from my best friend Kevin! Don't we have a great time talking and playing together?"

Jeff got up. He put his dollar in his gold-car bank. He read his card one more time. "To someone special—I love you very much!" Carefully he put his card in his drawer with all his other treasures.

"I guess I'll never know who sent me the valentine," Jeff said. "But it's made me think of all the people who love me in a special way. I sure am lucky to be so loved."

Who knows? Maybe that is the very reason Jeff's dad didn't sign his valentine card to Jeff this year.

ABE LINCOLN'S FUNNY STORIES

by Abraham Lincoln and others

(Abe Lincoln had something in common with school children today. He loved to hear and tell funny stories. Let older students tell a funny joke or two. Share some of these that Abe heard or told. Then let the students try writing or making up their own jokes and riddles.)

Last night I heard a story about Daniel Webster. One day at school he broke one of the rules. I don't know which one. Anyway, the teacher caught him. He called him up to his desk so he could punish him. . . the old-fashioned way— smacking his hand with a ruler.

Now Dan knew his hands were pretty dirty. So on his way up to the teacher's desk, he spit on the palm of his right hand. He wiped it off on the side of his pants.

"Give me your hand, sir," said the teacher sternly.

Daniel put out his partly cleaned right hand.

"Daniel," said the teacher. "If you can find another hand in this room as filthy as that, I will let you off this time!"

Instantly, from behind his back came Daniel's other hand. "Here it is, sir," he said.

"That will do, Daniel," said the teacher. "You may take your seat."

Adapted from *Joe Miller's Jests* (1845). Lincoln changed "Dr. Wall" to Daniel Webster.

One day Mr. Lincoln was walking along a dusty road in Illinois. A stranger in a carriage drove up from behind.

"Sir," called Mr. Lincoln as the carriage passed by, "will you take my overcoat into town for me?"

"Why, yes," said the stranger. "But how will you get it back again?"

"Oh," said Mr. Lincoln, "why now, I intend to stay in it."

Adapted from *Sam Weller's Jest Book* (1837) and told on Lincoln.

One day the crowds kept calling for Mr. Lincoln to come out and speak to them. After a while, tall Mr. Lincoln and his short wife stepped out onto a balcony. Mr. Lincoln made this short speech.

"Here I am, and here is Mrs. Lincoln. That's the long and the short of it."

Reported by H.J. Raymond, in *Life and Public Service of Abraham Lincoln* (1865).

The other day, Mr. Lincoln was up not far from Kansas, with a friend or two. They saw a small stream. "What is its name?" Lincoln asked.

One of the passengers said, "It is called, 'The Weeping Water.' "

Lincoln's eyes twinkled. "You remember," he said, "the laughing water up in Minnesota, called Minnehaha? Well, gentlemen, it seems to me this should be called Minneboohoo."

Harper's Weekly, April 28, 1860.

"That reminds me of a fellow out in Illinois," said Mr. Lincoln. "He had better luck hunting prairie chickens than anyone in the neighborhood.

" 'How is it, Jake,' asked his neighbor, 'that you never come home without a lot of birds?'

"Jake grinned. 'Oh,' he said, 'I jes' go ahead an' git 'em.'

" 'Yes, I know; but how?'

"Jake leaned over close to his neighbor's ear, and said, in a whisper: 'All you got to do is hide in a fence corner an' make a noise like a turnip. That'll bring the chickens every time.' "

―――――――――――

"I went to the door because I heard the cries of children," said Mr. Lincoln's neighbor, Roland Diller. "There was Mr. Lincoln, walking by with two of his boys. Both of them were crying. 'Why, Mr. Lincoln, what is the matter with the boys?' I asked.

" 'Just what's the matter with the whole world,' Lincoln answered back. 'I've got three walnuts. And each of them wants two.' "

These stories are retold from *Abe Lincoln's Yarns and Stories.*

"How many legs does a mule have if you call a tail a leg?" asked Mr. Lincoln.

(The answer, of course, is four. Calling a tail a leg doesn't make it a leg. This riddle is from the Lincoln debates.)

A FLAG FOR GENERAL GEORGE

by Sandi Veranos

Someone knocked. Betsy Ross put her tape measure on the chair she was measuring for a new cushion cover. "Maybe it's a customer," she said. She went to the door.

"Uncle," said Betsy as she opened the door a bit and peeped around it. "Come on in. How nice of you to call." It was only after Betsy Ross opened the door completely that she saw that Uncle George Ross was not alone. "Please, do come in," she said.

In the living room, George Ross turned to Betsy. "Betsy," he said, "this is General George Washington, the commander of our army. And our friend Robert Morris."

Betsy Ross greeted the visitors.

"We have a job for you, Betsy," said Uncle George when they had all been seated.

"You do?" asked Betsy.

"We want you to make a flag," said General Washington.

"A flag?" asked Betsy. "I've never made a flag before. What kind of flag do you want?"

"It's to be a surprise," said Uncle George.

"We don't want anyone to know about it yet," said Robert Morris.

"Will you keep our secret?" asked General Washington.

"Of course," Betsy said.

"We are going to be a new nation soon," the men said. "And we need a flag for our country."

"Do you want a square flag? Or a rectangular flag?" asked Betsy.

"I have a picture of how we think our flag should look," said General Washington. He showed the picture to Betsy Ross.

"It will have stripes—seven red ones and six white ones," said Robert Morris.

"Thirteen in all," said Betsy.

"We want good strong colors," said General Washington.

"And a blue field in the upper left corner," said Uncle George.

"With thirteen white stars in a circle on the blue," said General Washington.

"Do the stars have to have six points?" asked Betsy Ross as she looked at the picture. "I'd like five-pointed stars better."

"Aren't they harder to make?" asked General Washington.

"I can do it," said Betsy. "I can cut them easily with my scissors."

"Then five-pointed stars it will be," decided General Washington. "The stars must be in a circle. Each colony in our new country must know it is important. If its star were not there, the circle on the flag would be broken."

"We will come by for the flag in a couple of days," said Uncle George as the three guests got ready to go.

"The flag will be ready," she said.

Betsy Ross wanted the new flag to be just right. She found the whitest cloth she had. Then she dyed part of it bright red and part deep blue. Carefully she cut the stripes, the stars, and the blue field. Then Betsy Ross picked up her needle and thread. She sewed and sewed, making sure each stitch was her very best.

At last the new flag was all done. "It's beautiful," she said.

"It's a fine flag," agreed General Washington, Robert Morris, and George Ross when they saw the flag Betsy had made.

"It will make the soldiers proud," said George Washington.

"When our flags fly on ships at sea, they will be easy to see," said Robert Morris. He was a shipping merchant. "And if a captain turns it upside down so other ships will know he needs help, the people who see it will know for sure it is not flying right and something is wrong. Then they will help."

"And all of our colonies will know it belongs to them. They are equally important parts of our new country," said Uncle George.

The three men took Betsy Ross' flag and told her good-by. A few days before they signed the Declaration of Independence, they showed the flag to members of Congress. "It's a proud new flag for a new country," said General Washington. And Congress agreed.

On July 4, 1776, the thirteen colonies became a new and independent nation.

Betsy Ross looked at the new flag fluttering in the breeze. "It's beautiful," she said. And she was truly proud.

MELISSA'S GROUNDHOG

by Sandi Veranos

"Do we have any groundhogs on our farm?" asked Melissa on a January morning.

"Yes," said Father. "But not today. It's much too cold. Groundhogs are all sound asleep in their homes under the ground at this time of the year."

"Where do ours live?" Melissa wanted to know. "By the barn? Or down by the creek? Or where?"

"Out in the pasture," said Father. "Why?"

"Groundhog Day is coming," said Melissa. "Do you think our groundhogs will come out and see their shadows? How do they know when it's time?"

"Good questions," said Mother.

"Very good questions," Father agreed.

"You know, Melissa," said Mother, "not so long ago people couldn't turn on the television and hear about the weather. They had to watch the sky and the earth around them. They tried to guess what the weather would be by what they saw."

"That's right," said Father. "And the idea of an animal seeing its shadow and going back to sleep has been around a long time. Long ago, farmers in Germany watched badgers. When German farmers came to America, they did not see badgers. They saw groundhogs. So they watched them instead."

"Let's watch our groundhogs. Could we?" Melissa wanted to know.

"We could try," promised Father.

Early on Groundhog Day, Mother called to Melissa. "Wake up, honey," she said. "The sun will be up before long. You want to see what the groundhog does, don't you?"

Melissa opened her eyes and sat up. "Put on warm clothes," Mother

said. "It will be cold out in the pasture."

Mother, Father, and Melissa took their camp stools. They found a spot by a tree. Father took his binoculars so they could see the groundhog up close without him being frightened.

They waited. Nothing moved in the field.

"I'm cold," said Melissa after awhile.

"I brought us some hot cocoa," said Mother. "And some nice warm sticky-buns are in the picnic basket."

"A winter picnic. What fun," said Father.

The warm gooey rolls tasted good. They chased the hunger away. The cocoa made Melissa feel warm and snuggly inside.

Still no groundhogs came. Melissa laid her head down in Mother's lap. Mother put the cloth from the picnic basket around her. Melissa was soon sound asleep.

They waited.

"I don't think we will see anything, do you?" asked Mother.

"No," said Father after awhile. "Maybe we should just go."

Mother was about to awaken Melissa when Father cautioned her. "Shh," he said, "Don't move. Stay still."

Mother looked. A head popped up out of a hole in the ground. "Melissa," Mother whispered.

"Look." She gave her daughter a little shake. Melissa opened her eyes.

"Shh," Mother warned her.

A groundhog climbed out of his hole. He wobbled about. Father let Melissa look at him with the field glasses. As she watched, the groundhog took a dive back into his hole.

"He must have seen his shadow," said Melissa.

"I guess he did," said Father. "The sun is shining. I see mine. And he's disappeared."

"And now we will have six more weeks of winter," said Melissa.

"Shall we watch the days on the calendar and see if he's right?" asked Mother.

And that's exactly what they did. Was the groundhog right? What do you think? Why do you think that?